# Revelatio

## BIBLE TRIVIA

1.

2.

3.

4.

5.

6.

7.

8.

## VIDEO DISCUSSION GUIDE

1. Briefly define the following terms:

   a. Belgic Confession

   b. revelation

   c. religion

   d. general revelation

2. Why is knowing the basic facts about what we believe just as important as having the right feelings or commitment?

3. General revelation in nature: You are outdoors in the mountains, looking at a sky full of brilliant stars. Or you are taking a hike through an autumn forest. Or you are watching a thunderstorm roar in over a lake. Think about a personal encounter with God's world that impressed you. What did it show you about God?

4. General revelation in history: Think of a recent event in your nation's history or your personal history. What did that event show you about God?

5. General revelation in conscience: Suppose you hurt someone at school by insulting her in front of her friends. That night you can't get to sleep. You begin to regret deeply what you did. How has God used your conscience to reveal himself? What has been revealed?

6. General revelation is nonredemptive, says Pastor Lew. It can't save us. Why not?

7. Imagine an isolated tribe in the dense tropical rainforests of Brazil. Members of this tribe have never heard the gospel. Yet they live by a strict moral code: People who are caught stealing have their hand cut off. Capital punishment is the penalty for murder. The tribe worships the sun, trusting it to provide them with food, prosperity, and long life.

   Where do you think this tribe got its sense of morality and its sense of the divine? Is this tribe religious?

   Can this tribe give the excuse that it has not been introduced to the one true God? Why or why not? What do Romans 1:19-20 and Article 2 of the Belgic Confession say about this?

   May we say with finality that this tribe is not saved? Why or why not? What implications are suggested for mission work?

# Special Revelation

## REVIEW QUIZ

(true/false)

_____ 1. The author of the Belgic Confession is Pastor Lew Vander Meer

_____ 2. The Belgic Confession was written during a time when Dutch Protestants were persecuted by Roman Catholics.

_____ 3. The Belgic Confession was written during the 1500s.

_____ 4. The word "revelation" means how we respond to God.

_____ 5. The nonredemptive display of God in the world is known as general revelation.

_____ 6. The three parts of general revelation are nature, history, and the Bible.

_____ 7. Everyone is exposed to God's general revelation.

_____ 8. General revelation alone cannot save us.

_____ 9. General revelation can help people understand who God is.

_____ 10. The word "religion" means to show or reveal.

## BIBLE TRIVIA

1.                          5.

2.                          6.

3.                          7.

4.

## VIDEO DISCUSSION GUIDE

1. How does special revelation differ from general revelation?

2. List four special ways that God revealed himself during Old Testament times. What's the main way that God's special revelation comes to us today?

3. What do we mean when we say a book of the Bible is "canonical"?

4. According to 2 Peter 1:20-21, what was God's role in the writing of Scripture? What was the role of its human authors?

5. Our church teaches that the Bible is authoritative, inspired, and infallible. What do these words mean? How do they affect the way you read and regard the Bible?

6. If Bibles were banned and you had absolutely no access to Scripture from this point on in your life, what difference might it make? What, if anything, would you miss? How might your life be changed?

# God's Word

## REVIEW QUIZ
(true or false)

_____ 1. Canonical books are those that are fortresses for the truth.

_____ 2. Special revelation tells people how to be saved.

_____ 3. Theophanies, voices from God, prophets, and miracles are forms of special revelation.

_____ 4. The Bible is God's general revelation.

_____ 5. Inspiration refers to the way the Bible writers got all excited and enthusiastic about their work.

_____ 6. The writers of the Bible pretty much copied down what God told them to, word for word.

_____ 7. The main way that God's special revelation comes to us today is through the Bible.

_____ 8. The three parts of general revelation are nature, history, and conscience.

_____ 9. General revelation is nonredemptive.

_____ 10. Only Christians receive God's general revelation.

## BIBLE TRIVIA

1.                            5.

2.                            6.

3.                            7.

4.                            8.

## VIDEO DISCUSSION GUIDE

1. Four Bible study tools that Pastor Lew mentions are

   •

   •

   •

   •

2. Define and give an example of each of the following:

   a. moralism or moralizing:

   b. historical-redemptive approach:

   c. reading in context:

   d. S.I.S.:

   e. literal vs. symbolic approach:

3. Practice

   a. Use a Bible concordance to track down the following:

   • the location of the parable of the rich man and Lazarus

   • a chapter in which Jesus refers to hell three times

   • an Old Testament passage about sharing your food with the hungry

b. What morals or "lessons" could you draw from the parable of the lost son while missing its main message? (Luke 15:11-32)

c. Look at the chapter in which the parable of the lost son is located. What precedes the parable that helps us understand its meaning? What is the context of this parable? How does this help us understand the parable?

d. What does this parable show us about God and the way that God is working to save his people (historical-redemptive approach)?

e. Are parables like the one about the lost son literal—that is, they mean exactly what they say—or are they symbolic—that is, they suggest meaning beyond what they actually say?

4. What helps you when you read and study the Bible? Maybe something that *you* do will help others. Please share any ideas.

# Apologetics

## REVIEW QUIZ
(fill in the blanks)

1. Special revelation comes to us mainly in _____.

2. Another word for saying that the Bible is "God-breathed" is _____.

3. One tool for studying the Bible is _____.

4. When we say that the story of the feeding of the five thousand only teaches us to share our food, we are guilty of _____.

5. Bible passages should not be taken out of _____.

6. The historical-redemptive approach to Scripture always asks what a passage tells us about _____.

7. Another principle of reading the Bible is S.I.S.: Scripture _____ Scripture.

8. Psalm 23 says that God makes us lie down in green pastures. This should be understood as symbolic, not _____.

9. The three parts of general revelation are _____, history, and conscience.

10. The confession of the church that pastor Lew often refers to is _____.

## BIBLE TRIVIA

1.                              5.

2.                              6.

3.                              7.

4.                              8.

## VIDEO DISCUSSION GUIDE

1. What were some of the things that Christians living in the first few centuries were accused of? What role did the "apologists" play?

2. What's meant by "the scientific method"? What happens when this method is applied to God?

3. How would you defend your faith against the accusation that because it cannot be conclusively "proven" to be true, it is therefore irrational and illogical?

4. Are one person's beliefs about God just as valid as another person's beliefs? Why or why not?

5. What point was pastor Lew trying to make with his story of the young person standing by his mother's casket and being asked if she loved him?

6. "Always be prepared to give an answer to everyone who asks you to give the reason for the hope that you have. But do this with gentleness and respect . . ." (1 Peter 3:15-16).

   - In what situations, present or future, might you see yourself possibly being asked why you are a Christian or why you believe in God?

   - Suppose one of your good friends doesn't believe in Jesus. One day your friend asks you, flat-out, why you believe in Jesus. What would you say?

# The Attributes of God

## REVIEW QUIZ
(true or false)

_____ 1. Defending one's faith is called making an apology.

_____ 2. Christians in the first few centuries after Christ were often falsely accused of wrongdoing by their enemies.

_____ 3. Augustine was a Roman emperor who often attacked Christians.

_____ 4. We can scientifically show that God exists and that everything in the Bible is true.

_____ 5. The Christian faith can be defended as logical and rational.

_____ 6. The Holy Spirit has to work in our hearts to give us faith in God.

_____ 7. Special revelation comes to us in nature, history, and our consciences.

_____ 8. Inspiration refers to the way that God "breathed" his Spirit into the Bible writers.

_____ 9. The historical-redemptive approach to the Bible always asks what a passage tells us about God and God's relationship to his people.

_____ 10. The entire Bible should be read as literally true.

## BIBLE TRIVIA

1.                          5.

2.                          6.

3.                          7.

4.                          8.

## VIDEO DISCUSSION GUIDE

1. Definitions

   • attributes:

   • God's incommunicable attributes:

   • God's communicable attributes:

2. Make a list of the communicable and incommunicable attributes of God. You may want to refer to Article 1 of the Belgic Confession.

3. How could knowing about God's incommunicable attributes help us? When, for example, might knowing that God is powerful and almighty be especially important to us?

4. How could knowing that we share certain attributes with God be helpful to us?

5. Although God reveals himself to us, we need to realize that God is also awesomely mysterious. As finite human beings, we cannot fully know who God is. Give some examples of times when you sense God's greatness and mysteriousness.

# The Trinity

## REVIEW QUIZ
(fill in the blanks)

1. The attributes of God are his _____ that he has revealed to us.

2. God's incommunicable attributes are ones that _____ _____.

3. God's communicable attributes are ones that _____ _____.

4-5. Two examples of God's incommunicable attributes are _____ and _____.

6-7. Two examples of God's communicable attributes are _____ and _____.

8. The belief that the Bible is true is ultimately based on _____.

9. The nonredemptive display of God in the world is called _____.

10. Although God does reveal himself to us, we need to realize that God is also awesomely _____. We cannot fully know who God is.

## BIBLE TRIVIA

1.                          5.

2.                          6.

3.                          7.

4.                          8.

## VIDEO DISCUSSION GUIDE

1. It's about 4 o'clock, and you just got home from school. An unfamiliar car drives up to your house, and two men get out and knock on your door. You're the only one home. You answer the door and discover that they are Jehovah's Witnesses. They begin to question your beliefs about God. You claim to believe in the Trinity, but they challenge you to prove it from the Bible.

   How would you respond? What Scripture passages would you direct them to?

2. Most people agree that the Bible presents three persons: Father, Son, and Holy Spirit. What, then, is the real issue?

3. Read Article 8 of the Belgic Confession. Use it to develop a simple definition of the word *Trinity.*

4. The best-known Christian creed in the world is the Apostles' Creed. Show how it is a trinitarian creed. Which member of the Trinity does the creed devote most space to? Why?

5. What difference does it make to you personally whether or not you believe the doctrine of the Trinity? Does it really matter? Explain.

# Election

## REVIEW QUIZ
(fill in the blanks)

1. The doctrine of the Trinity says that _____
   _____
   _____.

2. One example from the Bible where all three persons of the Trinity are mentioned is _____
   _____.

3. The key issue in the doctrine of the Trinity is that all three persons of the Trinity are _____
   _____.

4-5. The two types of attributes God has are
   _____ attributes and
   _____ attributes.

6. Special revelation comes to us today in
   _____.

7-9. General revelation is found in _____,
   _____, and _____.

10. When we say the Bible is inspired, we mean it is God-
   _____.

## BIBLE TRIVIA

1.                              5.

2.                              6.

3.                              7.

4.                              8.

## VIDEO DISCUSSION GUIDE

1. What is God's election? Explain the doctrine of election from both the Calvinistic and the "free will" perspective. Which explanation gives humans more control? Which view do you personally think is right? Why?

2. How do the following texts support the idea of election, of God's choosing some to be saved?

   • Ephesians 1:4-5

   • Romans 8:28-30

   • Matthew 24:22, 24, 31

   • John 15:16

3. Do you think the teaching of election is fair? Why or why not?

4. Does God choose to send some people to hell? And if so, isn't this cruel?

5. How do you know if you're elect?

6. What does TULIP stand for?

# The Image of God

## REVIEW QUIZ
(multiple choice)

_____ 1. God choosing who will be saved is called the doctrine of (a) free will (b) election (c) Calvinism (d) predestination.

_____ 2. The two main schools of thought regarding election are (a) Calvinism and capitalism (b) Calvinism and free will (c) Calvinism and communism (d) Calvinism and Lutheranism.

_____ 3. The Calvinists believe that (a) we choose God and then he chooses us (b) God chooses us and then we choose him (c) nobody chooses; our salvation just happens (d) none of these.

_____ 4. Proof for the Calvinist view of election is found in (a) Psalm 23 (b) John 3:16 (c) Ephesians 1:4-5 (d) the creeds but not the Bible.

_____ 5. People know they're elect because (a) they believe in Jesus (b) God tells them so in his Word (c) they ask their pastor (d) they live good lives.

_____ 6. Which of the following is *not* a communicable attribute of God: (a) loving (b) holy (c) infinite (d) wise (e) good?

_____ 7. The doctrine of the Trinity says that there are/is (a) three persons, three Gods (b) one God in three similar persons (c) one God (the Father) and two persons who are less than God the Father (d) one God in three distinct persons (e) none of these.

_____ 8. Which of the following does *not* describe the Bible: (a) inspired (b) general revelation (c) special revelation (d) infallible (e) authoritative.

_____ 9. The belief that the Bible is the true Word of God is ultimately based on (a) recent scientific findings (b) hard historical evidence (c) faith (d) none of these.

_____ 10. Which of the following is *not* a part of general revelation: (a) the Bible (b) nature (c) conscience (d) history.

## BIBLE TRIVIA

1.                          5.

2.                          6.

3.                          7.

4.                          8.

## VIDEO DISCUSSION GUIDE

1. Think of someone you know who probably isn't a Christian. Describe some of that person's positive qualities and gifts. According to Pastor Lew, what enables people like this to do good and to be loving, productive human beings?

2. What do we mean when we say we—and all people—are "images of God"?

3. Read Genesis 1:26-27, 31. How did humans resemble God at creation?

4. When sin entered the world, did people lose the image of God? How does the crumpled paper analogy help explain what happened?

5. Should Christians reflect God differently than non-Christians? Why or why not? See Ephesians 4:20-24 and Colossians 3:9-10.

6. What impact can the "image of God" have on the way you see yourself and others? On your attitudes and behavior? Please complete the following statements:

- Because all people are made in the image of God, I should . . .

- Because I am made in the image of God and am becoming a new person in Christ, I should . . .

7. Believing in the biblical teaching that people are imagebearers of God has some wide-reaching implications, especially for the ethical or social issues our society faces. For example, how might this belief affect your view of capital punishment? What other issues might be affected by believing that all people are made in the image of God?

# Sin

## REVIEW QUIZ
(true/false)

_____ 1. To be made in God's image means to be like him in some ways.

_____ 2. When God created people, they were already imperfect imagebearers of God.

_____ 3. Unbelievers have lost all traces of the image of God.

_____ 4. As imagebearers, Christians ought to reflect God differently than non-Christians.

_____ 5. Christ is working in Christians to restore the image of God to what it once was.

_____ 6. Respect for life should result from believing that people are imagebearers of God.

_____ 7. The doctrine of election says that God chooses to save some of humankind, all of whom other-wise be condemned because of their sin.

_____ 8. The "T" in TULIP stands for total perfection.

_____ 9. Calvinists believe that we choose God and then God chooses us for salvation.

_____ 10. People know they're elect because they live good lives.

## BIBLE TRIVIA

1.                          5.

2.                          6.

3.                          7.

4.                          8.

1. Definitions

    a. original sin:

    b. actual sins:

    c. sins of omission:

    d. sins of commission:

    e. guilt:

    f. pollution:

2. Name the six stages in the "process of sin."

3. At which of the six stages do you think sin occurs?

4. Think of some recent sin in your life. Did it follow these six stages?

5. On a scale of one to ten, with ten being very seriously and one not at all, how seriously does our society in general regard sin?

6. Why not simply avoid the topic of sin? Why study something so negative and depressing?

# Salvation

## REVIEW QUIZ
(true/false)

_____ 1. Being curious about something evil is sinful.

_____ 2. Lust or strong desire to do something wrong is usually considered sinful.

_____ 3. Calvinists believe that all people are born sinful.

_____ 4. Original sin is the first sin we commit.

_____ 5. Sins of omission are sins we have committed but should have omitted.

_____ 6. Guilt refers to our legal standing before God.

_____ 7. Total depravity means that every aspect of our being is tainted with sin.

_____ 8. The doctrine of the Trinity says that there is one God in three distinct persons: Father, Son, and Holy Spirit.

_____ 9. All people are imagebearers of God.

_____ 10. Unlike non-Christians, Christians reflect God's image perfectly.

## BIBLE TRIVIA

1.                          5.

2.                          6.

3.                          7.

4.                          8.

## VIDEO DISCUSSION GUIDE

1. What is it like to feel alienated from God because of your sin? Why is it so important to our salvation to experience the alienation that sin causes?

2. God's calling us is the first step in the process of salvation (see 1 Peter 5:10 and 1 Thessalonians 2:12). As you think about your own spiritual journey, what are some of the ways God has called or is calling you?

3. What is the second step of salvation, and what does it mean (see Acts 16:13-15)?

4. What is the third step of salvation, who performs it, and what are its two parts (see Acts 3:19)?

5. Must we all "be converted" to be saved? If conversion is a turn-around in our lives, must we be able to point to a specific time when we were converted? Explain.

6. You are at a Christian youth convention with other teens from your church and hundreds of other kids from all around the country. At the last big meeting of the conference, a guest speaker delivers a powerful appeal for people to come to the front and give their lives to Jesus Christ. You find yourself strangely moved. Something inside is tugging at you, urging you to join the others who are coming forward. At the same time you feel reluctant because you know you already are a Christian and have already given your life to Christ.

In this situation, what would you probably do? Why?

7. Describe the fourth step along the way of salvation (see Romans 5:1-2, 9).

# Sanctification

## REVIEW QUIZ
(fill in the blank)

1. _____ is the first step in the process of salvation.

2. Preaching, Bible reading, and the witness of parents and friends are examples of God's _____ calling.

3. _____, the second step, is the name of the process whereby God makes the dead heart of sinners come alive.

4-5. _____, the third step, involves a sudden or gradual turn in one's life. It includes faith and _____.

6-8. In the fourth step, known as _____, God declares us _____ because of _____ _____.

9. The doctrine of _____ says that God chooses to save some of humankind, all of whom would otherwise be condemned.

10. The six stages in the process of sin are knowledge, curiosity, desire, lust, decision, and _____.

## BIBLE TRIVIA

1.                              5.

2.                              6.

3.                              7.

4.                              8.

## VIDEO DISCUSSION GUIDE

1. Describe the fifth step in the process of salvation (see 2 Corinthians 5:17). Who performs this step (see 1 Corinthians 6:10; Ephesians 4:22-24)?

2. Recall the story (with two different endings) Pastor Lew told about the boy who bounced his ball through the window of his neighbor's house. What does this story have to say about our reason for "doing good"?

3. Can a person be a Christian without doing anything that could be called "good" in God's sight? Can we have faith but not have a Christian lifestyle that goes with it?

4. In many places the Bible tells us that our new lives in Christ should "bear fruit" and give evidence in our daily lives of the faith we claim to have (see, for example, 1 Corinthians 12:27-31; James 2:14; Ephesians 4:20-32; Galatians 5:22-26). Using these passages and your own ideas, work with one or two others to create a profile of what we as new people in Christ should be like. Write your ideas on a large sheet of paper—add some creative touches to your poster too.

5. What's the point of Pastor Lew's tory about the soldier and the meeting in the train station?

6. OK, so you've heard about the need to be like Jesus and to show that we love him by doing good to others. If you're willing, list two or three "good works" that you could realistically do in the next week or so out of gratitude for what God has done for you. Be as specific as possible.

# Perseverance of the Saints

## REVIEW QUIZ

(true/false)

_____ 1. Sanctification means getting rid of the pollution in our lives and living the new life in Christ.

_____ 2. Sanctification is something that we have to do on our own.

_____ 3. One of the reasons we "do good" is to help pay God back, in part, for the gift of salvation.

_____ 4. If we don't do any good works, then our faith is dead.

_____ 5. People who are Christians can't help but do good deeds for Jesus.

_____ 6. Faith and repentance are part of the regeneration process.

_____ 7. Calvinists believe that God, not people, begins the salvation process.

_____ 8. In justification, God declares us not guilty on the basis of our own good acts for Jesus.

_____ 9. The first three steps in the process of salvation are calling, curiosity, and conversion.

_____ 10. The fourth and fifth steps in the process of salvation are justification and sanctification.

## BIBLE TRIVIA

1.

2.

3.

4.

5.

6.

7.

8.

## VIDEO DISCUSSION GUIDE

1. Review the differences between Calvinists and some "free will" churches, using the acronyms TULIP and CURB. Write a brief definition behind each letter.

T

U                                    C

L                                    U

I                                    R

P                                    B

2. Read the following passages that support the idea that God will never let us go: John 6:37-40; Romans 8:29-30; 1 Corinthians 1:8; Philippians 1:6. Which passage speaks most clearly and powerfully to you about your "eternal security" in Christ?

3. Doesn't the saying "Once a Christian, always a Christian" contradict Hebrews 6:4-6, which says that it is impossible for those who "have once been enlightened" and who have fallen away to be brought back to repentance? Explain.

4. One objection to believing the saying "Once a Christian, always a Christian" is that it could lead to a kind of "lazy" Christianity in which people pretty much do as they please, since they're saved anyway. How would you respond to this?

5. A friend of yours confides that her older brother, John, has lost all interest in Christianity. He used to be very active in the church and was a strong Christian. But after he got married, he rarely went to church, and now he says he no longer believes in Jesus. Her parents are very upset about the situation and pray daily for him. Your friend is worried about her brother. She wonders what you think about the situation.

    a. Does this example contradict the doctrine of the perseverance of the saints? Why or why not?

    b. What would you say to your friend?

6. Reflect on your feelings about the saying "Once a Christian, always a Christian." When would knowing this be especially comforting to you?